Pilgrimage and Possession

Conversion in the Writings of St Teresa and St John of the Cross

SISTER EILEEN MARY SLG

SLG PRESS
Convent of the Incarnation
Fairacres Oxford

ISBN 0 7283 0097 4
ISSN 0307-1405

ACKNOWLEDGEMENTS

We wish to thank Search Press for permission to quote prose passages from *The Complete Works of St John of the Cross,* translated by E.A. Peers.

Thanks are also due to Sheed and Ward Ltd for permission to quote liberally from *The Complete Works of St Teresa,* translated by E.A. Peers.

We are grateful to Dr. E.W.Trueman Dicken for permission to print his translated copy of the sketch of *The Mount* by St John of the Cross.

PREFACE

This study of the teaching of St John of the Cross and St Teresa of Avila does not attempt to cover the full range of their writings. Little mention will be found of two of St John's major works, *The Living Flame of Love* and *The Spiritual Canticle*, while *The Life* and *The Way of Perfection* of St Teresa are only used to supplement her teaching in *The Interior Castle*. There are two reasons for this. Firstly, there is a good deal of duplication in the works of both writers, while secondly, I decided it would be more useful here to concentrate on the actual steps along the way as they are set out in *The Ascent of Mount Carmel, The Dark Night of the Soul* and *The Interior Castle*.

But does that way, as expounded by traditional Western mystical theology, really do justice to the relationship between spiritual and earthly which is implicit in the Resurrection? I had recognized something of what that relationship could mean in the holy earthiness of the *staretsi* whom I had met in Romania and Serbia, rooted as it was in the fullness of the Trinitarian faith and nourished by the Scriptures and the teachings of the Fathers. For the first thousand years of the Church's existence this had been the common mystical tradition of East and West. After that, the effects of the great Schism were to cause the Western Church to develop its own emphases in doctrine and mystical theology, in which over-definition—among other things—led to departmentalism. If, for instance, we did not know that St John of the Cross must have shared in the sacramental and liturgical life of his Church we might well think that public worship had nothing to do with the ascent of Mount Carmel. Yet in the writings of St John and St Teresa indications of the older, undivided tradition can be found hidden behind the terminology and outlook of scholastic philosophy and Counter-Reformation theology. The maxim of St John with which the present study begins is one sign that the living vision was still to be found in its dynamic fullness in the Church of sixteenth-century Spain.

The three circular diagrams (see pp. 23, 24, 26) can be seen as a form of icon which attempts to show something of the scope of the action of the three Persons of the Trinity within creation, within the Church's worship and in the gradual sanctification and transformation of the human being.

I am indebted to the German Lutheran Community of Imshausen for my introduction to *I-Ching* diagrams and their application to Christian life and worship. That Community has developed its vision in many ways of its own, but here the diagram is used as a key to unlock St Teresa's Mansions, showing that the creative Movement at the heart of our lives was discerned from afar by Chinese philosophers some thousands of years before a Spanish nun picked up her pen in 1577 to describe her vision of the Interior Castle. More can be learned of this philosophy from *I-Ching or Book of Changes* (an English rendering of the Richard Wilhelm translation, Routledge & Kegan Paul, 3rd edition, 1968).

My thanks are also due to the late Fr Gilbert Shaw who opened up the treasure-house of Carmelite teaching to my generation of the Sisters of the Love of God, helping us as Anglicans to enter into our heritage in the one great tradition of Christian spirituality. This study then reflects what I have made my own; it is a personal reading of two great doctors of the universal Church and I make no claim to authority for my interpretation of their works.

CONTENTS

MOUNT CARMEL

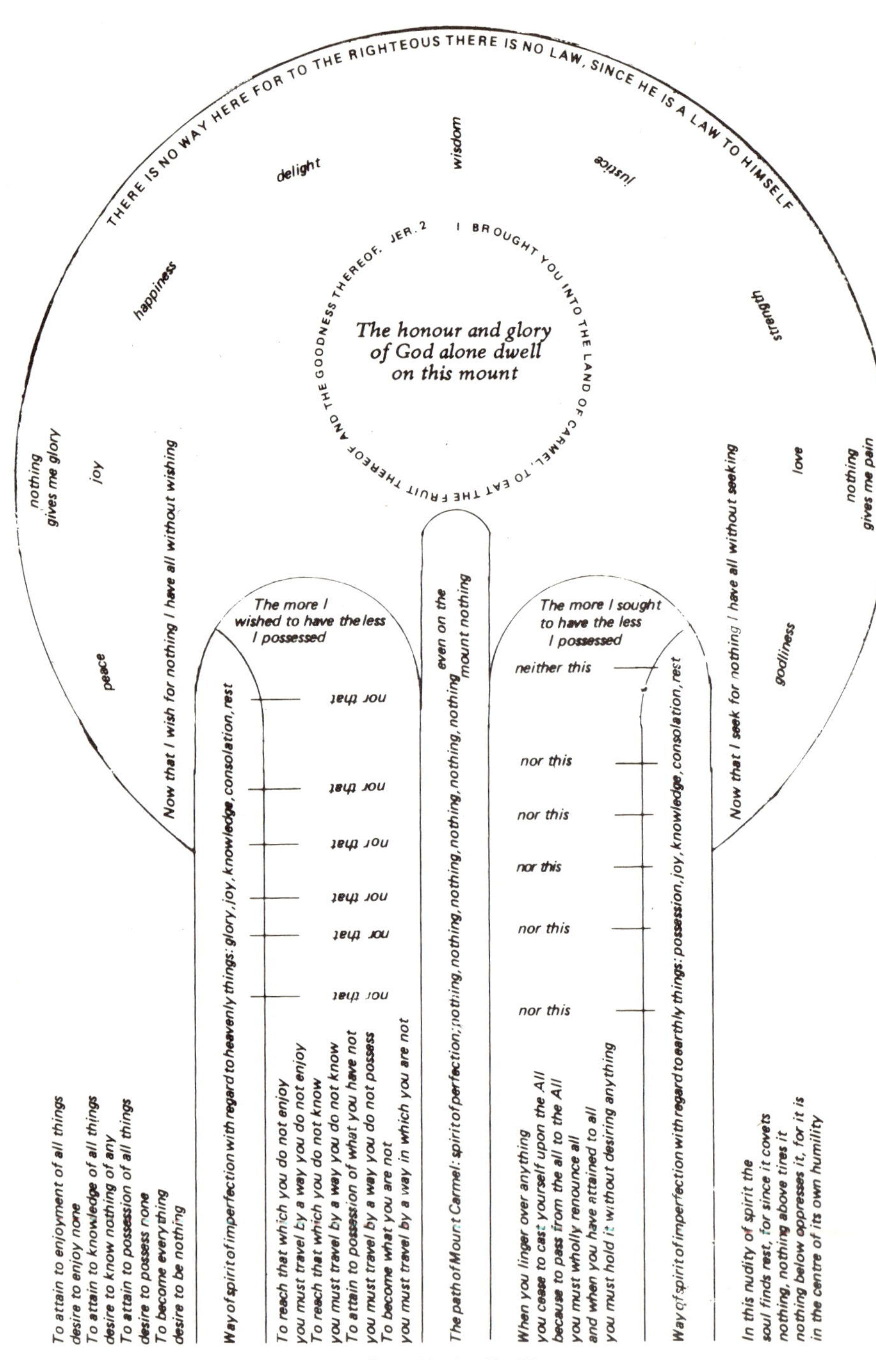

Reproduction of the original sketch of Mount Carmel by St John of the Cross, unaltered apart from regularization of the lines and translation of the Spanish and Latin words

CHAPTER I

Being and Becoming

> Mine are the heavens and mine is the earth; mine are the people, the righteous are mine and mine are the sinners; the angels are mine and the Mother of God, and all things are mine; and God Himself is mine and for me, for Christ is mine and all for me. What then dost thou ask for and seek, my soul? Thine is all this, and it is all for thee. Despise not thyself nor give thou heed to the crumbs which fall from thy Father's table. Go thou forth and do thou glory in thy glory. (*Spiritual Sentences and Maxims, Complete Works*, St John of the Cross, vol.iii, trans. E. A. Peers.)

This passage illustrates the twofold theme of possession and pilgrimage which underlies the teaching of St John of the Cross. There is a unity of the spiritual and material worlds which man is created to possess and to enjoy. Ultimately his state will be nothing less than deification through his union with God, a transformation which will be effected through a lifetime's education and training. 'For the whole business of attaining to union with God consists in purging the will from its affections and desires; so that thus it may no longer be a base, human will, but may become a Divine will, being made one with the will of God.' (*Ascent*, III. xvi. 3.)

So the way to possession of the heights of Mount Carmel is by means of a pilgrimage in which all experience great or small is gradually converted and taken along to that place of union. The physical world has an integral part to play as the raw material of experience and growth revealing both the love and beauty of God and also something of the hardness and terror of the way. The beauty of the world as such was not an obstacle to St John and it was no Manichee who could thus express its sacramental nature in his poetry:

O woods and thickets
Planted by the hand of the Beloved!
O fresh green meadows,
Enamelled with flowers,
O tell me, has he passed your way?

Scattering a thousand graces,
He passed swiftly through these groves
And, simply by his glance,
Lighting on them as he passed,
Left them clothed with beauty.

The obstacle lies rather in the weakness of the traveller who, forgetting how much farther there is to climb, sits down under the trees, or worse, tries to possess the countryside for himself. William Blake wrote:

He who bends to himself a joy
Does the wingèd life destroy;
But he who kisses the joy as it flies
Lives in Eternity's sunrise.

St John expresses the same truth in his own words in Book III of *The Ascent:*

> He will find greater joy and recreation in the creatures through his detachment from them, for he cannot rejoice in them if he look upon them with attachment to them as to his own . . . He will also acquire, in his detachment from things, a clear conception of them, so that he can well understand the truths relating to them, both naturally and supernaturally . . . This man, then, rejoices in all things—since his joy is dependent upon none of them—as if he had them all. (III. xx. 2-3)

So the material world has solidity and worth as a work and instrument of God, and this includes the human person with his earthly senses as well as his intellectual and moral powers. St John is defining in terms of the Scholastic philosophy of his day the 'altogether' relationship of the total manhood. His psychology, derived from his religious and cultural background, is not that of the twentieth-century Western world; nevertheless the psychological complexity of the human person is recognized and taken into account. The reader has to disentangle for himself the universal truths of his teaching from the particular terminology and imagery in which they are expressed. Initially he has to enter into the world of St John in which man is seen as a being made up of body and soul. The lower levels of the soul are closely associated with the bodily senses which mankind shares with the animals, and to these is joined a reaction to the memory of joy and pain, which St John calls imagination. For example a person may run away from a barking dog which has no intention of biting him, because as a child he was knocked down by one. The senses, through the imagination, are reacting to a memory of pain. At these bodily, sensual levels, joy, grief, hope and fear–four of the most potent human emotions–are experienced as passions in response to external stimuli.

The 'higher' levels of the soul, which St John sometimes calls spirit, contain the more complex faculties of memory, understanding and will. Here joy, hope, grief and fear are more solid sentiments which may be centred round the most noble traits in man, such as prayer, patriotism, religious culture, love of family or of a particular work for God. Yet on the height of Mount Carmel the words are written: 'The honour and glory of God alone dwells on this mount'. The *nada* of the way up involves the acceptance at every level of the truth that all things are relative; detachment from them is painful in proportion to the intensity with which they are clutched at and clung to. The way is dark because the traveller cannot see the good that awaits him. Yet it must be repeated that it is not love of the creatures which is the obstacle but the human tendency to make creatures into idols.

There is little mention in St John's works of the rich liturgical and sacramental life of the Counter-Reformation Church of sixteenth-century Spain. That is so much taken for granted that only the weaknesses of popular religion are exposed. Enough remains even today in the baroque churches of southern Europe with their elaborate architecture, statuary and extra-liturgical devotions to make the visitor feel that the author's strictures were probably justified. He writes of those who were Christian and devout, but in his opinion only half-converted, ' . . . they burden themselves with images and rosaries which are very curious; now they put down one, now take up another; now they change about, now change back again; now they want this kind of thing, now that, preferring one kind of cross to another because it is more curious. And others you will see adorned with relics and tokens like children with trinkets.' (*Dark Night*, I. iii. 1) Such aids may be used in moderation, but the substance of devotion 'makes use only of what suffices for that end and grows weary of this other kind of multiplicity and curiosity'.

All this is relevant to our more streamlined age with its own material and immaterial toys and props which also have to be kept in proportion. The appeal of St John for every generation lies in his basic simplicity and concern to reorientate all human desire into that desire for God planted within the human soul at baptism but overlaid by a mass of lesser desires at every level of its being. As life proceeds these lesser desires may harden into a conditioned pattern which the Spirit of God can penetrate only with difficulty. Therefore the way of deconditioning will be inevitably stringent if all desire is to die and rise again as servant rather than as master of the human soul. St John is asking, 'How much do you want God? How much do you want to live from your true self?' He is pointing out that the usual path to simplicity is by means of a lifetime of work and suffering, many digressions, false starts and weakenings of purpose which are described in great detail in his treatises on *The Ascent of Mount Carmel* and *The Dark Night of the Soul*.

Yet it must not be forgotten that the end is joy and a largeness of vision which is given in proportion as other things do not get in the way. In the original map of Mount Carmel which St John drew for his spiritual daughters (see opposite p. 1), the narrow way gives access to the whole of Mount Carmel. Here there are none of the foothills and gradations which appeared in later versions of the map. 'Now that I wish for nothing I have all without wishing. Now that I seek for nothing I have all without seeking'– and that 'all' includes peace, joy, happiness, delight, wisdom, justice, strength, love and godliness–those things which most people desire but do not know how to find.

St John of the Cross is above all the mystic of night and unless a person submits the night and its shadow within himself to the action of the Spirit he will never find freedom. No mystic way which ignores or tries to bypass the darkness of evil and suffering and the confusion which is an indispensable part of spiritual growth can ultimately allow man to be at home within a universe which in itself seems to be so mysterious and unideal. For St John the only security lies in a dark faith in a God who cannot be defined according to human modes of understanding. So the *Ascent* opens with the image of a man setting out by night from a known country along a path he cannot understand towards a God whom he cannot see.

> These three parts of the night are all one night; but like night itself it has three parts. For the first part which is that of sense, is comparable to the beginning of night, the point at which things begin to fade from sight, and the second part, which is faith, is comparable to midnight which is total darkness. And the third part is like the close of night, which is God, the which part is now near to the light of day. (I. ii.5.)

On this journey St John distinguishes between the things which man can do, aided by the grace of God, and those which must be done in him, over which he has no control. The four or five stages in a person's journey which he discusses under the headings of the active and passive nights of the senses and of the spirit are not a neat scheme for spiritual advancement which can be weighed and measured but rather a description, infinitely varied in each person, of what is liable to happen when Christian life and prayer are taken seriously. In some measure all four processes go on together throughout life, yet on the whole it is the senses which soonest loose their hold, and the more subtle, spiritual part of man which needs the longest and deepest purification and reorientation to the one-pointed desire for God. It would be a mistake to use this teaching of St John as a yardstick for one's own spiritual progress, yet he does help to explain experiences which one may have passed through without understanding, to give reassurance for the past and present and a fresh vision of possibilities for the future.

Two further points must be made before the reader begins the Ascent with St John. Nowadays his 'nights' are sometimes explained away as psychological rather than spiritual states. It is true that the spiritual experience may be accompanied by depression, a sense of worthlessness or claustrophobia arising from physical and chemical or emotional causes, but this is not the whole of the story. A 'night' as defined by St John of the Cross involves some element, however slight and hidden it may be, of love and trust in a God who is active in, and also beyond, the cloud in which the depressed person may live (see *Dark Night*, I. ix). So the whole process is described in terms of a pilgrimage in which the footsteps taken into the night, however small and faltering they may seem to be, are in fact adventures of love demanding from the outset a great deal of courage and trust on the part of the traveller.

The second point is best expressed in St John's own words:

> And since this instruction relates to the dark night through which the soul must go to God, let not the reader marvel if it seem to him somewhat dark also. This, I believe, will be so at the beginning when he begins to read; but as he passes on, he will find himself understanding the first part better, since one part will explain another. And then, if he read it a second time, I believe it will appear sounder. (*Ascent*, Prol. 8.)

The unfolding can only be gradual as the reader grows in the capacity to understand and the obedience to follow, and this process will continue throughout life. St John does not write for the spiritual dilettante but for the humble persistent seeker after God, who knows that there is always more to discover and to learn in the realm of the spirit.

CHAPTER II

The Way in The Ascent of Mount Carmel *and* The Dark Night of the Soul

ST JOHN OF THE CROSS says in *The Dark Night of the Soul* that he is writing for beginners. Yet the first seven chapters show that his readers already have considerable experience of the life of the Church. They fast and pray and use the sacraments (I. iii; vi. 4), they are given to good works (I. i. 2), they read, study and listen to sermons (I. iii. 1; vi. 6) and are in fact thoroughly respectable members of the Christian establishment. Yet in his exposition of the symptoms of pride, wrath, avarice, luxury, gluttony, envy and sloth St John shows that it is just as possible for desire to fasten on to holy things as on to more material objects, and this can be seen in his map of the way (see opposite p. 1). There is no difference between the two side paths of the 'way of spirit of imperfection with regard to heavenly things' and the 'way of spirit of imperfection with regard to earthly things'. It is true that both paths penetrate into the mountain but they are sealed off from the full freedom and richness of life which is to be found through the naked path of the middle way.

It is necessary to turn to *The Ascent of Mount Carmel*, Book I, chapters ii-xii, to see why this is so. St John describes the tyranny of lesser desires which weary, torment, darken, defile and weaken the person and impede the action of the Spirit of God within. He calls the initial stage of the cure for this condition the active night of the senses, something which can only be entered into by acts of the will, and this is discussed in chapters xiii-xv. His object is to begin to break the the tyranny by recommendations which may seem more suited to the harsh psychological climate of sixteenth-century Spain than that of twentieth-century Western Europe where many people have to learn the positive use of the senses before they can discipline them. This in fact is implicit in the first of these recommendations, where St John says that the pilgrim should have 'an habitual desire to imitate Christ in all that he does . . . conforming himself to His life; on which life he must meditate so that he may know how to imitate it, and to behave in all things as Christ would behave' (I. xiii. 3). It is clear from the New Testament that Jesus' senses were not dulled either by misuse or by lack of use. In every parable he revealed his delight in the natural world, in the sacramental nature of simple human actions, in the intricacy of creation. So for us the entrance into the night of the senses may involve learning to sit still, perhaps on the sea-shore, watching the infinite variety of texture and colour, smelling the scent of sea and seaweed, listening to the cry of the gulls, letting the sand run through our fingers, giving thanks and praise for what is offered to our senses as free gift. Against this use of the senses there is surely no law. What has to be renounced for the love of Christ is 'every pleasure that presents itself to the senses, *if it be not purely for the honour and glory of God*' (my italics). It is a commonplace fact that all of us for most of the time are being conditioned by the newspapers we read, the television programmes we watch, the advertisements that seduce us at every tube station, designed as they are by experts in psychological techniques to appeal to the gluttony, avarice, lust, envy, anger in man. This is the given situation of our time and culture, and for St John the cure would have consisted not in shutting the eyes and the mind to these outside influences, but in keeping alive the power of discernment and choice by positive acts of the mind and will. However, so insidious is the conditioning and so hidden the seduction that the cure has to be a drastic one. St John, faced by the equivalent allurements in his own culture, countered them with his famous aphorisms which may sound stringent and life-denying to modern ears:

> Strive always to choose, not that which is easiest, but that which is most difficult;
>
> Not that which is most delectable, but that which is most unpleasing;
>
> Not that which gives most pleasure, but rather that which gives least;
>
> Not that which is restful, but that which is wearisome;
>
> Not that which gives consolation, but rather that which makes disconsolate;
>
> Not that which is greatest, but that which is least;

Not that which is loftiest and most precious, but that which is lowest and most despised;

Not that which is a desire for anything, but that which is a desire for nothing;

Strive not to go about seeking the best of temporal things, but the worst.

Strive thus to desire to enter into complete detachment and emptiness and poverty, with respect to that which is in the world, for Christ's sake.

And it is meet that the soul embrace these acts with all its heart and strive to subject its will thereto. For if it perform them with its heart, it will very quickly come to find in them great delight and consolation, and to act with order and discretion. (*Ascent*, I. xiii)

It is a process of re-education which many would reject today as psychologically unsound and harmful. Yet it is worth mentioning that if the first seven of these aphorisms are applied, even to any secular learning situation, whether the purpose be to drive a car, acquire a foreign language or master the intricacies of a computer, it is probable that the one who follows them will make the quickest and most thorough progress.

We have seen that at this stage St John recommends active meditation of a kind similar to that of St Ignatius Loyola, based on Gospel scenes and the life of Christ (*Ascent*, I. xiii.3). Such meditation should continue as long as possible 'in order to dispose and habituate the spirit to spirituality by means of sense, and in order to void the sense, in the meantime, of all the other low forms and images, temporal, worldly and natural' (II. xiii.1). It is a door, a sign of goodwill and an invitation to God to enter and to take the initiative. He will respond to the invitation by invading the person at a deeper level in a mode of communication inaccessible to the senses, experienced initially as boredom and incapacity and later as infused strength in the heart and will. All this is dealt with in great detail in chapters viii-xi of the first book of *The Dark Night* which can be supplemented by reading *The Ascent*, Book II, chapters xiii-xv. St John explains how this state—which he calls the passive night of the senses—is to be distinguished from that of someone who is merely tired of God and prayer through 'sins and imperfections, or from weakness and lukewarmness, or from some bad humour or disposition of the body' (*Dark Night*, I. ix.1). A dark night is not to be correlated with indigestion.

The three signs of goodwill which he gives are distinguished by the thread of love which runs through the suffering, resulting in a willingness to be in darkness and passivity for as long as God considers it to be necessary (*Dark Night*, I. ix). He stresses the danger of a person reaching round at such a time for new techniques and tools of meditation to help himself, and so hindering the next stage of his spiritual evolution. He should rather be like someone whose face is being made up by another person . . . 'If the sitter were to move because he desired to do something he would prevent the painter from accomplishing anything and would disturb him in what he was doing' (*Dark Night*, I. x. 5).

What then should he be doing in his time of prayer? 'What [such persons] must do', says St John, 'is merely to leave the soul free and disencumbered and at rest from all knowledge and thought . . . contenting themselves with no more than a peaceful and loving attentiveness toward God and in being without anxiety, without the ability and without desire to have experience of Him or to perceive Him' (*Dark Night*, I. x. 4). In other words, communication comes through a steady and patient gaze into a darkness within, which although it remains dark, becomes pregnant with life, bringing a communication of Spirit to the spirit of man in a manner hitherto not known. Although mental prayer may be impossible, simple acts of love condensed into one or two words, are not. St John says that

> the soul is now like one to whom water has been brought, so that he . . . is no longer forced to draw the water through the aqueducts of past meditations and forms and figures. So that as soon as the soul comes before God, it makes an act of knowledge, confused, loving, passive and tranquil, wherein it drinks of wisdom and love and delight. (*Ascent*, II. xiv. 2)

The passive night of the senses should lead to a further conversion of the whole life as God works upon the disordered desires at a deeper level than anyone could do for himself. In the alternation of experiences of darkness and emptiness with those of strength and tenderness, he begins to learn humility and reverence for God and his fellow-men, so that desire begins to fade away almost of its own accord:

> [The soul] loses the strength of its passions and concupiscence and it becomes sterile, because it no longer consults its likings. Just as, when none is accustomed to take milk from the breast, the courses of the milk are dried up, so the desires of the soul are dried up. (*Dark Night*, I. xiii. 3)

In chapters xi-xiii St John shows how the romanticism has begun to go out of religion, one is more capable of 'eating bread with crust' and of enjoying 'the food of robust persons'.

Yet this reorientation of the senses is lifelong and we can never assume that the work is done. It is a gradual process of de-conditioning whereby the subject becomes more capable of of making free choices as against the conditioned reflexes derived from inner and outer psychological pressures. So his capacity for good or evil becomes greater. St John calls this state 'the active night of the spirit', for the purgation takes place at a more profound level, in the memory, understanding and will, which in the psychology of the day were regarded as the higher faculties of the soul. The twentieth century may well prefer to place these things within the context of the unconscious, influenced as they are by a thousand currents from the past and from the environment, of which the subject may know little or nothing. Yet because at the conscious level the memory has some knowledge of God's goodness it can face the future in hope and trust; because the understanding has learnt something of the knowledge that comes from faith it can go further in that dark way of knowing; because the will has begun to learn what it is to discipline the senses for the love of God it can act out of deeper charity. An illustration can be given from Ida Görres' book on St Thérèse of Lisieux, *The Hidden Face.* Thérèse, having lost her mother by death and her beloved elder sister Pauline to Carmel, was suffering from what today would be diagnosed as a nervous breakdown:

> In constant reiteration, in ever more emphatic form, Thérèse expressed by a whole language of gesture one and the same emotion: 'I want Pauline, I must go to Pauline; I don't want her to be away; I can live only with her; I will fall sick, go mad, die without Pauline; none of you can help me; I don't want the rest of you to help me . . .' She could not understand herself, of course (how could we

expect her to be capable of such understanding?); she was terrified by the incomprehensible forces that overwhelmed her. From all her sisters' whisperings . . . she had to assume that the most horrible of all fates had come upon her: diabolic possession. Nevertheless, we believe that a decision must have taken place deep within her when, in the midst of her direst distress, the saving grace of the vision of Mary shone upon her. We believe that at this point Thérèse was confronted with a temptation, for all that it was hidden in the unplumbed depths of the soul. For here she was confronted with alternatives, and the second of these alternatives was the perilous one. She could accept the offered comfort, the new support and protection. That is, she could abandon her wild despair over what she had lost, could really carry out the unendurable renunciation within the core of her ego, could release the hand of Pauline and reach across the irrevocable gulf for the hand of the Blessed Virgin. Or—and this was the other possibility—she could cling to her despair, could hold tight to her neurosis, could maintain her protest, stubbornly persist at all costs in the sinister attempt at blackmail which this disease represented.

Such decisions take place not by deliberate processes of thought, but far below the strata of thoughts and words, by a lightning-like opening or closing of the core of being [my italics] .

Precisely here we see the child destined to be a saint; not that the miracle happened to her, but that she obeyed it. (pp. 79-80)

In the night of the spirit, 'far below the strata of thoughts and words, by a lightning-like opening of the core of being' the active decision was made in obedience, rendering the psychological compensations for which the child had been crying out no longer necessary. How then can our memory, understanding and will be trained so that at the moment of trial they too will make the obedient and life-giving choices? St John reiterates that the basic disposition must be a readiness to go forward in dark faith, treating the undeniably good gifts of the inner life as relative aids on the way. Immaterial possessions—and their name is legion—such as one's cherished modes of approach to God, spiritual insights and charismatic experience must be recognized as only 'the crumbs which fall from the Father's table', to be received with gratitude, used and then left behind, for they are not of the very essence of reality and at the moment of trial they may let one down.

Modern readers of Book II of *The Ascent*, in which St John amplifies these points in terms of the spiritual and psychological phenomena of his day, may find his examples wearisome and naive, and it is true that they have to be 'demythologized' before the message comes through. Yet the counterparts of the visions and locutions to which he refers occur in present-day experience. For instance he writes with disapproval of those who 'have the desire to know things by supernatural means'. This does not mean that one should not pray to the Holy Spirit when guidance is needed, but that the flash of inspiration which may well follow such a prayer must be submitted to the natural reason and to

> an evangelical doctrine and law which are quite sufficient for the soul's guidance, and there is no difficulty or necessity that cannot be solved and remedied by these means, which are very pleasing to God and of great profit to souls; and such great use must we make of evangelical doctrine and reason that, if certain things be told us supernaturally, whether we so desire or no, we must only receive that which is in clear conformity with reason and evangelical law.
>
> (*Ascent*, II. xxi. 4)

He goes on to say that 'in all our anxieties, trials and difficulties there remains for us no better and surer means than prayer and hope that God will provide for us, by such means as He wills' (*Ascent* II. xxi. 5). In other words, we are being warned about taking short cuts and ascribing to the authority of the Holy Spirit what may well come from the hidden desires of the unconscious or from human powers of intuition. We should rather remain poised on the event, waiting to see how God will reveal his purpose through time, space, persons and the revealed Christian law and Gospel, and in particular through the science and practice of the Cross. Therefore one who is in earnest should have a soul-friend or confessor to whom he should submit his spiritual experiences, even though he may feel a complete fool in doing so (*Ascent*, II. xxii. 18, 19).

Book III, chapters i-xv deal in much the same way with the cleansing, healing and right use of memory by means of the theological virtue of hope. To cling to particular memories, whether they be good or bad, is to lessen one's capacity to act in the present. If particular experiences as they occur are allowed to drop gently into the memory and the subject remains unflurried and open as one person and event after another confronts him in his daily life, the Holy Spirit will draw out from the memory the appropriate response as and when it is needed (*Ascent*, III.ii. 11, 12). Western technological man is so used to twisting time and matter out of their natural rhythms that he does not realize how well obedience to these rhythms can work in cultures which have not lost their simplicity. We strain ourselves battling against them instead of working with them.

Healing of the memories will not come through dwelling on them or struggling with their causes, but only through putting the situation into God's hands whenever the interior storm comes to the surface, and riding out the tempest (*Ascent*, III. iii. 4). We may recall again how it was only when Thérèse was ready to drop her memories of how things had been and how she felt they ought to be that God's grace, mediated through the smile of the Virgin, could penetrate the cloud and bring her healing.

In these chapters on memory there is also a useful paragraph on intercession (*Ascent*, III.ii. 10). It is unnecessary for the interceder to remember lists of people and details of their needs, although he might once have known them. All he need do is hold himself open to the Spirit who at the appropriate time will bring to the surface of his mind those for whom he should be praying, who may sometimes even be 'others of whom he has no knowledge nor has ever heard'. This can be illustrated by a story told in our own day of Father William of Glasshampton who, with a pile of requests for intercession before him on his prayer desk, drew out for attention this one or that as the Spirit moved him, while essentially bringing the whole pile with him into the worship of God.

As faith and hope are summed up in charity, so the activities of memory and understanding find their fulfilment in the work of the will which is also charity. Behind all the detail—sometimes so complicated—of St John's teaching, is the great law of love.

And now that we have to treat of the active detachment and night of this faculty, in order to form it and make it perfect in this virtue of the charity of God, I find no more fitting authority than that which is written in the sixth chapter of Deuteronomy, where Moses says: Thou shalt love the Lord thy God with all thy heart and with all thy soul and with all thy strength. Herein is contained all that the spiritual man ought to do, and all that I have here to teach him, so that he may truly attain to God, through the union of the will, by means of charity. For herein man is commanded to employ all the faculties and desires and operations and affections of his soul in God, so that all the ability and strength of his soul may serve for no more than this . . .

(*Ascent*, III. xvi. 1)

St John recognizes four passions of the soul and affections of the will–joy, hope, grief and fear–which can either be a strength, if they are focused on God, or an obstacle, if they are clung to for their own sake. He has already dealt with the passions of the soul which are the immediate reactions to the stimuli of the senses and which may come and go, sometimes with great rapidity. But the affections of the will are more solid sentiments. They are drawn to areas of sensitivity around which one may have lived for half a lifetime: unhealed memories, griefs as sharp and poignant as when they were first experienced, fears arising from the basic drive for self-preservation, physical and spiritual joys of the past still clung to in the present. One thinks of characters in fiction who have come to be dominated by the sentiment itself–a Mr Micawber or a Mrs Gummidge, fixed respectively in hope and grief–and these are by no means untrue to life.

Originally St John intended to discuss each of the four affections of the will in turn, but in the book as it has come to us, he has in fact dealt only with joy, and has not even finished that. If, however, as he says, when one of these affections is purified so are all the others, perhaps this incompleteness does not matter. He begins then in chapter xvii what will prove to be a long and detailed dissertation extending over the remaining twenty-eight chapters of the *Ascent*.

Joy may arise from six kinds of good things or blessings, namely: temporal, natural, sensual, moral, supernatural and spiritual. Of these we shall speak in their order, controlling the will with regard to them so that it may not be encumbered by them and fail to place the strength of its joy in God. To this end it is well to presuppose one fundamental truth, which will be as a staff whereon we should ever lean as we progress . . . This truth is that the will must never rejoice save only in that which is to the honour and glory of God . . . and anything that has nought to do with this is of no value and profit to man.

(*Ascent*, III. xvii. 2)

Let us take heart however. None of this disallows our natural joys so long as they are placed under the dominion of God's law and love. In fact these should lead to a greater unification of prayer and life as we confide more and more of our possessions to the safe-keeping of God.

This again envisages a lifelong process which at the same time opens the door to God's further action within the core of being, the essential 'I' who lives far below the possessions and movements of the soul. In *The Dark Night of the Soul*, Book II, St John discusses what he calls 'the passive night of the spirit', a darkness in which the faith and hope by which one has been sustained cease to operate in relation to the things of God and only the will goes on functioning in an arid way. The previous purgations had really touched only the outside, acting as a preparation for what must come to pass if the soul is to become mature in love. An example may again be taken from the life of St Thérèse of Lisieux, speaking to one of her sisters during her last painful illness. The sister reported afterwards: 'She admitted something to me which surprised me strangely: "If you only knew the darkness into which I have been flung! I don't believe in eternal life; I think after this life there will be nothing more. Everything has vanished for me." But she added afterwards, "All that I have left is love." ' St John says of this state of purgation that in it the soul 'is conscious of the complete undoing of itself in its very substance' (*Dark Night*, II. vi. 6), and that on the whole it has to last for many years if it is to be really effective, since there are intervals of relief when the soul comes up, as it were, for air (ibid. vii. 4). It is not difficult to imagine such experiences coming to St John in his imprisonment, to St Thérèse suffering from the hallucinations of severe tuberculosis or to a prisoner today in a concentration camp; yet in a measure every Christian nowadays who has not turned his back on the world is liable to feel something comparable. For involvement in our generation's spiritual and moral dilemmas alongside and within a Church which can no longer give definitive answers may produce a sense of the absence of God in those most deeply committed to him. St John uses the image of Jonah swallowed into the darkness of the fish's belly, the image used by Christ of his own descent into hell (Matt. 12: 40); whatever inapprehensible darkness may be, he knew it also. As Christ rested in the tomb, so 'in this sepulchre of dark death [the soul] must needs abide until the spiritual resurrection which it hopes for' (*Dark Night*, II. vi. 1). As Christ rose out of the grave, so too, St John promises, when night has done its work within a man, he will be transformed into the image of Christ as a log of wood is transformed and takes the properties of the fire with which it is united (ibid. II. x. 1).

So the language at the end of the second book of *The Dark Night* is the language of the divinisation of the human soul. In *The Spiritual Canticle* and in his poems St John expresses something of what that can mean.

CHAPTER III

The Service of Love

DESPITE the universality of the journey, it may still seem that St John's approach is individualistic, centred round the odyssey of particular souls. What is the service of such a pilgrimage to the world as a whole?

The following quotation from a living author is given here in order to draw out in modern language themes which are implicit in St John's teaching, such as the value of suffering as a catalyst for love; the coinherence of the individual with the world and with the whole of mankind; and worship as the way through to life, and not only for the one who prays. Petru Dumitru, the author of *Incognito*, does not write from a Christian standpoint, yet Stefan, the hero of his novel, speaking from the prison cell in which he has been held and tortured, is nonetheless a type of the Redeemer:

> The world may be finite or infinite, round or square, this way or that way, but we must love it. It suffers and we must seek to relieve its suffering, through ourselves and through others, teaching it to love and to be happy in the love it learns. Our bodies and our whole being flow towards death; but matter flows towards life, and life towards consciousness, and consciousness towards love and rapture. The species flows towards each one of us, and through each of us, before we return to dust; it seeks by suffering to reach beyond the individual: from unconsciousness to consciousness, from primitive impersonality to personality, and from personality to sanctity which is its transcendence, a higher impersonality, the gift of the 'me' acquired, enriched and harmonised by so much labour. And beyond this there are heights of which it is not opportune to speak, since language has its bounds.
>
> . . . .
>
> Above all I formed the habit of praying in all circumstances, even the most humble and by convention most inappropriate to the worship of God. I taught myself not to confine my love to one aspect of the world more than another, not to ignore hateful and repulsive things. I

taught myself to love evil in sacred terror before the wrath and mystery of the world, which is cruel and suffers, both victim and torturer, terrible and unhappy . . . Apathy—which is the suffering of God, the painful slumber of God—drags us back: towards civilised man, then primitive man, then the animal, then the plant, each level drawn towards the one below. But worship draws us upwards; and if the burden grows heavier as we yield to it, the triumph grows no less as it is gained, or as it is granted to us. We can conquer all things, freely choose our conquests, reckon with all things, knowing that every victory and every choice is a miracle. (chapter 30)

If this is true, then Christian mystical theology dare not point to a Platonic type of ascent which in its solitary approach to God transcends the body and the material as something coarse and unclean. A superficial reading of St John of the Cross and of many another Christian mystic may give this impression, but in the Judaeo-Christian revelation mankind is bound together in the solidarity of life, while the created universe itself 'waits with eager expectation for God's sons to be revealed' (Romans 8:22). The saint who claimed the heavens and the earth as his possession did not turn his back on the struggle that this solidarity involved. So, in the last year of his life, after he had been deprived of office by his enemies in the Order, St John wrote, 'And where there is no love put love and you will find love . . . ' (*Letters,* xxii). If the love, not only of the saints but of every Christian, can penetrate below the surface to the currents of life and death, it will release springs of energy for the healing of the nations and for those individuals in trouble or despair whom perhaps they will never know in this life. The wills of men cannot be controlled by prayer but the spiritual atmosphere in which decisions are made will be influenced by it. It is a form of service not easily to be discovered except through the nights of sense and spirit, experienced perhaps in sickness, poverty, old age or worldly disgrace. For then at last the mutable world is known for what it is, a precious gift and sign, but ultimately only the raw material for love.

CHAPTER IV

The Pattern

WE HAVE SEEN that St John of the Cross presents the Christian way as a pilgrimage, as the ascent of a mountain. In *The Interior Castle*, the most systematic of her works, St Teresa uses the imagery of exploration, of making one's way through a castle which contains a series of 'Mansions' (cf. John 14:2). These are arranged not in a consecutive sequence but variously, 'some above, others below, others at each side, and in the centre and midst of them all is the chiefest mansion where the most secret things pass between God and the soul' (*Interior Castle*, p. 202). Although St Teresa writes only of seven mansions, she says that the outside ones in particular have 'not just a few rooms but a very large number' (literally, 'a million'). So there is not a systematic method of entry into the castle but something much more haphazard and free. 'Since God has given it [the soul] such dignity, it must be allowed to roam through these mansions–through those above, those below and those on either side. It must not be compelled to remain for a long time in one single room' (p. 208).

A single visit is not sufficient; ' . . . thenceforward you may serve Him by going to these Mansions again and again till He brings you into the Mansion which He reserves as His own' (p. 350). So although there is a 'way' it is perhaps a spiral rather than a direct route, moving gradually towards the centre but involving much exploration, experiment and consolidation as more and more of oneself is brought under the control of God's love.

St Teresa does not give a systematic account of the makeup of the human being, but it must be remembered that she often follows St John of the Cross in using the word 'soul' to describe its more spiritual aspects, where St Paul would more properly have spoken of the 'spirit'. Nevertheless, she is aware that spirit and soul are not the same thing:

> It is possible to make observations concerning interior matters, and in this way we know that there is some kind of difference, and a very definite one, betweeen the soul and the spirit, although they are both one. So subtle is the division perceptible between them that sometimes the operation of the one seems as different from that of the other as are the respective joys that the Lord is pleased to give them. It seems to me too that the soul is a different thing from the faculties and that they are not all one and the same. (p. 333)

This is an important distinction if the respective messages from body, soul and spirit are not to become hopelessly confused in the judgement of the one who prays.

There is a recognition in St Teresa's writings that in our relationship with God some aspects of our nature respond more quickly than others. For instance, the praying spirit may leap ahead while the intellect, emotions and senses remain outside needing to be enticed into the Castle:

> What is the purpose, do you suppose, of these inspirations . . . and of these messages which are sent by the soul from its innermost centre to the folk outside the Castle and to the Mansions which are outside that in which it is itself dwelling? Is it to send them to sleep? No, no, no. The soul, where it now is, is fighting harder to keep the faculties and senses and everything to do with the body from being idle than it did when it suffered with them . . . It is quite certain that, with the strength it has gained, the soul comes to the help of all who are in the Castle, and, indeed, succours the body itself. (p. 347)

Again one notes that there is no Platonic transcendence of the spirit over the more earthly parts; ultimately we shall be transformed as a unity.

It must be admitted that it is not easy in any of St Teresa's writings to disentangle the central message from her comments and asides. Not only are the assumptions, standards and social patterns of sixteenth-century Spain very different from those of twentieth-century England, but Teresa wrote in a hurry, jotting down her thoughts as they came, repeating herself, excusing herself as a woman for writing at all, always keeping a wary eye on the Inquisition and its reactions. So although her writing is vivid, human and full of common sense, it is not always a model of clarity.

A thread is needed to help one steer a path through the maze and this may be found in the mysterious interrelation of the rhythms of the spiritual and material worlds. Each has its own particular mode of operation but one illuminates the other, so that there are few mystical writers who do not use natural images as icons of spiritual states. St John and St Teresa are no exceptions. The passage of night, the sunlight striking a diamond, the flowing of water, the transformation of the chrysalis into a butterfly are only a few of the images used by the Carmelite writers.

> In all the things that have been created by so great and wise a God there must be many secrets by which we can profit, and those who understand them do profit by them, although I believe that in every little thing created by God there is more than we realize, even in so small a thing as a tiny ant. (*Interior Castle*, p. 236)

In the ancient Chinese book of philosophy known as the *I-Ching* there is a succinct account of God's action in nature through the rhythms of night and day and of the seasons of the year, and this can be used as a guide to the spiritual path as it is described in *The Interior Castle*:

> God comes forth in the sign of the Arousing; he brings all things to completion in the sign of the Gentle; he causes creatures to perceive one another in the sign of the Clinging (light); he causes them to serve one another in the sign of the Receptive. He gives them joy in the sign of the Joyous; he battles in the sign of the Creative; he toils in the sign of the Abysmal; he brings them to perfection in the sign of Keeping Still. (*I-Ching*, Book II. ch. 1. p. 268)

Diagram I shows this movement of God's action in the cycle of the year which is mirrored in the passage of day and night. Below the east-west line the seed is exposed to the powers of *Yin*, the dark, compact soil which is made up of the bodily remains of millions of other lives. Above the line is the life of the individual plant, growing, flowering and coming to fruition under the light of the sun in the creative powers of *Yang*. At the threshold where *Yang* and *Yin* meet there is an area of change and conflict. God, unknown in his essence, works from outside the natural order, but is known on earth through his energies within it. All this has great significance when applied to the spiritual life of the Church and that of individuals.

So in the *I-Ching* scheme as it will ultimately be applied to

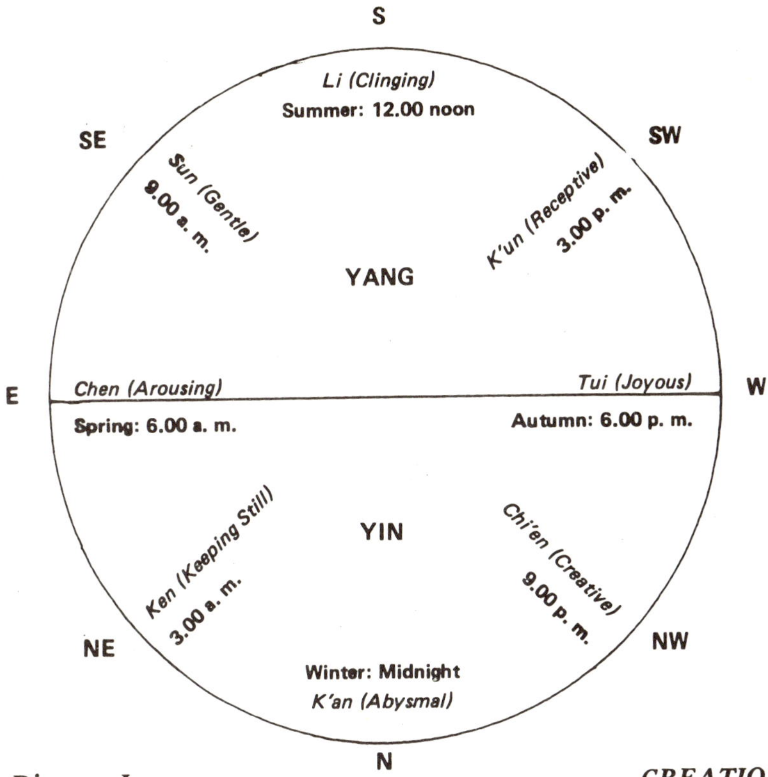

Diagram I *CREATION*
I-CHING, Sequence of Later Heaven or Inner-world Arrangement

The Interior Castle, the circle is entered between the south-west and the west as the parent plant produces its seed, with the old *serving* the new life; as autumn and evening approach there is the *joy* of fruition; when the new seed falls into the ground, *Yang* and *Yin* meet in *creative* tension; in the darkness of winter God himself works upon the seed in the *abyss*; in the night before the dawn it *lies still* while he perfects it. (Compare the last three points with the active and passive nights of St John.) The seed is *aroused* by the rays of the sun at dawn to develop the new life which is latent within it. The plant grows to completion under the *gentle* breezes of spring and takes its place within the whole interrelating pattern of nature. The flower opens itself to the sun, light *clings* to it making it visible to other creatures; it *receives* fertilization and so produces new seed in its turn. It is not difficult to see the classic pattern of mystical theology—purgation, illumination and union—even within the cycle of the natural order.

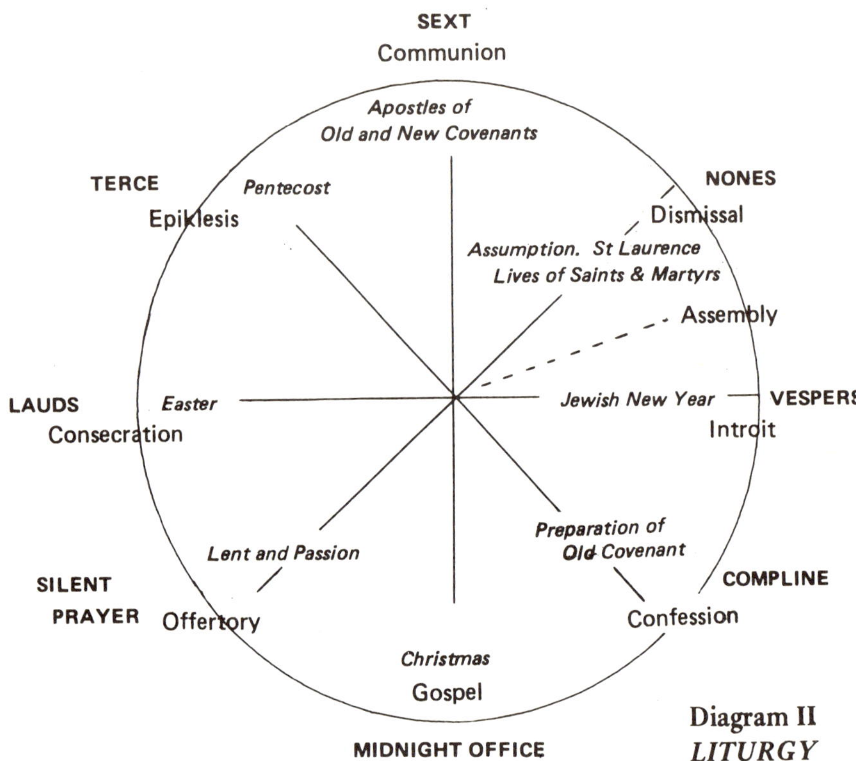

Diagram II
LITURGY

Diagram II shows how the Church has baptized these rhythms in the cycle of its annual feasts and fasts, a pattern which is reproduced in miniature in its daily Offices and in the actions of the Eucharist. The ground is now the Scriptures and tradition, the whole history of salvation as it is set out in the pages of the Old and New Testaments. The year begins with the Jewish New Year in September when the Church once again begins to recapitulate the mystery of Redemption. From then until Christmas is the period of the Old Testament, of the Law and the

Prophets, leading on to Advent and the immediate preparation for Christmas. It is then that Christ the incarnate Word enters into the circle, and his human life of mission, death and resurrection is re-enacted in liturgy and Scripture during the period from Christmas to Easter. The feasts of Easter and Pentecost celebrate the Church's entry into the new life of union with God through the work of the Spirit. Inevitably this leads on to the missionary apostolate which is celebrated at the height of summer in the feasts of St John the Baptist and St Peter and St Paul, and to the more complete service of the deaths of the saints and martyrs observed in the feasts of the Assumption and St Laurence. Similarly, one can see how this rhythm is celebrated in the Church's Hours of Prayer which somewhere in the world are being perpetually offered, as well as in the movements of the Eucharist. So the Church as a whole sanctifies natural times and seasons by pouring out the Word of God upon them through the Psalter, the Scriptures and its whole liturgical life.

All this is taken for granted in St Teresa's writings and it is assumed that the individual's prayer is based upon this rich heritage. Speaking of those in the sixth Mansion who say that they can no longer meditate upon the Mysteries of our Lord's life, she says, 'A man will not be right, however, to say that he cannot dwell upon these mysteries, for he often has them in his mind, especially when they are being celebrated by the Catholic Church.' (*Interior Castle*, p. 307). If it were not so we should look in vain for the mutual relationship of the individual and the corporate which in fact is the 'ground' of Diagram III. In the early stages the new Christian is absorbed into the religious culture, receiving life from the collective tradition. Gradually or suddenly, Christ becomes known to him as a living Person and this is his Christmas. He is then drawn into the mystery of death and resurrection in Christ through his daily life in which he experiences the gifts of the Spirit. All this is the personal history and adventure which he brings as his specific contribution to the life of the Church. The primary experience is of course unique, yet growth in capacity and understanding will be endless. Therefore, as St Teresa pointed out, there will be many a return to the Mansions that one has visited before, although, one may hope, to different and richer rooms. Yet the total

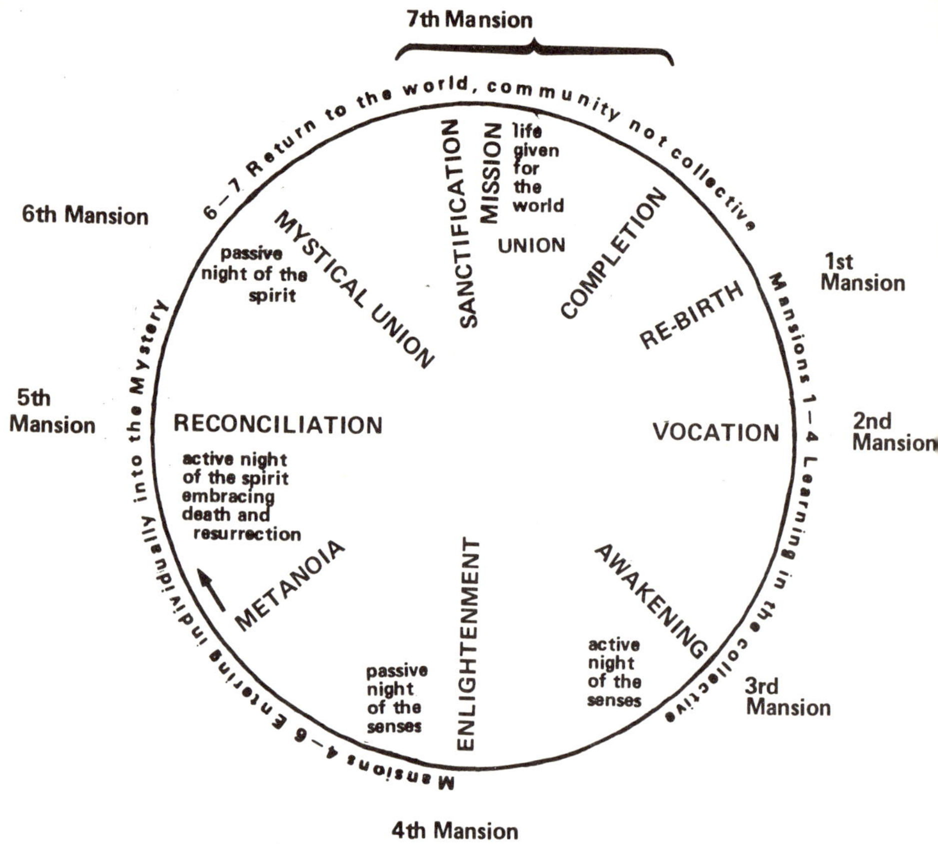

Diagram III *SPIRITUALITY*

movement should be one that gradually curves towards the innermost rooms of the Castle where God himself dwells in the heart of the Christian.

What then is the nature of that union? Despite the many mystical gifts that she herself had received, St Teresa knew it to be a union of wills in love rather than a matter of mystical absorption. And this, as she was fond of pointing out, is open to the humblest Christian. St Teresa usually writes of Christian living and Christian prayer together, moving from one to the other, explaining what is appropriate or likely to happen in each Mansion. Yet for her every experience of prayer was a pure gift and a miracle which might or might not be granted. This did not matter. The ultimate gift was the 'spiritual marriage' which was consummated for her in a vision of the risen Christ who 'told her that it was time she took upon her His affairs as if they were her own and that He would take her affairs upon Himself' (p. 334). It was a union of mutual trust and reliance but not one in which the unique human personality became swamped in the Deity, although there is one particular image in the seventh Mansion which might seem to suggest this.

Diagram III also shows the approximate relationship of St Teresa's Mansions to the Nights of St John of the Cross, although there are differences of interpretation. St Teresa stresses the happy, creative and miraculous elements of the spiritual journey; her imagery is dominated by the Sun shining in the heart of the Castle, overshadowed only by the clouds of sin. St John's habitual home is a wholesome night from which he sometimes emerges with great power and sweetness, but one senses nevertheless a little distrust of the day. These temperamental differences influence the way in which each experiences life and prayer, but the difference may be one of vocation too. In any case, if one wants to gain a comprehensive view of Carmelite spirituality, it is necessary to hold the teaching and insight of both saints together.

CHAPTER V

The Castle

THE MOST CONCISE description of this Castle is given in a letter by an old friend of St Teresa, Fray Diego de Yepes. He writes that God showed Teresa 'a most beautiful crystal globe, made in the shape of a castle and containing seven mansions, in the seventh and innermost of which was the King of Glory, in the greatest splendour, illumining and beautifying them all. The nearer one got to the centre the stronger was the light; outside the palace limits everything was foul, dark and infested with toads, vipers and other venomous creatures.' (*Interior Castle,* Introd. p. 188).

Each Mansion represents a richly complex point of polarization in the spiritual life and therefore its many rooms are entered in a variety of ways which include prayer, active asceticism and acceptance of the suffering that life brings. Reference to the various diagrams, it is hoped, will help to build up a picture of that rich complexity in terms of colour and feeling to illuminate St Teresa's own words.

FIRST MANSIONS: DEATH AND REBIRTH

This lies between the Receptive and the Joyous in the *I-Ching* circle, being the point at which the parent plant brings forth new seed and dies in its birth. It is linked in the cycle of the Office with Nones which traditionally is associated with the death of Christ and by implication with that of his saints and martyrs whose blood gives life to the Church. In one way or another a person has been receptive to some influence, has aroused himself from 'paralysis' and entered the collective of the Christian family. This is symbolized in the Eucharist by the moment of Assembly when the people of God enter the church building and become a community differentiated but not separated from those outside. For an individual, only a strong desire and much courage will provide the impetus necessary for entering the Castle and for going on when one has got inside. 'As far as I can understand', St Teresa says, 'the door of entry into this Castle is prayer and meditation', and she points out the need from the beginning for an elementary form of mental prayer. But when the new Christian enters he finds the outer rooms dimly lit and that he has brought in with him venomous creatures from outside.

> It is as if one were to enter a place flooded by sunlight with his eyes so full of dust that he could hardly open them. The room itself is light enough, but he cannot enjoy the light, because he is prevented from doing so by these wild beasts and animals, which force him to close his eyes to everything but themselves. (*Interior Castle*, p. 210-211)

These creatures include a too great occupation with worldly affairs, fears of what others may think and say, and fear for one's own safety and well-being. All this arises not from humility but from cowardice. True humility and courage will be gained by keeping the vision large and by not settling down for too long in any single room, even in that of self-knowledge.

> Believe me, the soul must sometimes emerge from self-knowledge and soar aloft in meditation upon the greatness and the majesty of its God . . . we shall reach much greater heights of virtue by thinking upon the virtue of God than if we stay in our own little plot of ground and tie ourselves down to it completely. (p. 208)

If one is to be able to 'gaze at the castle and enjoy its beauty . . . [he] will be well advised, as far as his state of life permits, to try to put aside all unnecessary affairs and business' (p. 211). Scattered throughout St Teresa's writings are pieces of advice on how the self can be gently disengaged from these things and attracted to the things of God through prayer and prayerful activities.

> It used also to help me to look at a field, or water, or flowers. These reminded me of the Creator—I mean, they awakened me, helped me to recollect myself and thus served me as a book. (*Life*, ix. p. 55)

> You will find it very helpful if you can get an image or picture of this Lord—one that you like—not to wear round your neck and never look at but to use regularly whenever you talk to Him, and He will tell you what to say. (*Way of Perfection*, xxvi. p. 109)

> It was not usual with me to suffer from aridity: this only came when I had no book, whereupon my soul would at once become disturbed and my thoughts would begin to wander. As soon as I started to read they began to collect themselves and the book acted like a bait to my soul. Often the mere fact that I had it by me was sufficient. Sometimes I read a little, sometimes a great deal, according to the favour which the Lord showed me. (*Life*, p. 24-5)

However, if one cannot do any of that,

> At such times the soul must render the body a service for the love of God, so that on many other occasions the body may render services to the soul. Engage in some spiritual recreation, such as conversation (so long as it is really spiritual), or a country walk . . . Sweet is his yoke, and it is essential that we should not drag the soul along with us, so to say, but lead it gently, so that it may make the greater progress.
>
> (*Life*, p. 70)

SECOND MANSIONS: VOCATION

St Teresa devotes only one chapter of *The Interior Castle* to this Mansion as she has already written on the same theme in the *Life*, chapters xi-xiii, and in *The Way of Perfection*, chapters xx-xxix. It is now September in the *I-Ching* circle, the time of the ripening of the seeds and the harvest. The joy of fruition is celebrated in the evening Office of Vespers, while in the Eucharist the entry of the priest during the singing of the Introit hymn symbolizes man's vocation to be the high priest of creation. With the acceptance of Christian vocation we have entered farther into the Castle. We can now 'hear' God speaking to us, not directly, but through the collective tradition:

> I do not mean by this that He speaks to us and calls us in the precise way which I shall describe later; His appeals come through the conversations of good people, or from sermons, or through the reading of good books; and there are many other ways, of which you have heard, in which God calls us. (*Interior Castle* p. 214)

She cites illnesses and trials, and truths which dawn upon us in prayer. Helping one's soul to remain in prayer is like breaking in an unruly colt; the faculties may be lured along, not driven.

> Remember that many years have passed since it went away from its Spouse, and it needs very careful handling before it will return home. We sinners are like that: we have accustomed our souls and minds to go after their own pleasures . . . until the unfortunate soul no longer

> knows what it is doing. When that has happened, a good deal of skill is necessary before it can be inspired with enough love to make it stay at home; but unless we can gradually do that we shall accomplish nothing. (*Way of Perfection*, p. 110)

So a definite time each day should be given to God in prayer, something which requires much strength and resolution.

> Since we have resolved to devote to Him this very brief period of time . . . let us give it Him freely, with our minds unoccupied with other things and entirely resolved never to take it back again, whatever we may suffer through trials, annoyances or aridities. (ibid. p. 98)

Yet she is not rigid:

> . . . we must not be considered as taking it back if we should fail to give it Him for a day, or for a few days, because of legitimate occupations or through some indisposition. Provided the intention remains firm, my God is not in the least meticulous; He does not look at trivial details; and, if you are trying to please Him in any way, He will assuredly accept that as your gift. (ibid. p. 98)

She gives more teaching about prayer in these outer Mansions. She would agree with the Jesuits that one must build up an image of Christ without, before seeking him within; otherwise the inward gaze may reveal only the self. Her method is simple. In *The Way of Perfection* she suggests the use of the imagination to picture our Lord standing, at this stage, not within but beside the one who prays. 'I am not asking you to think of Him or to form numerous conceptions of Him, or to make long and subtle meditations with your understanding. I am asking you only to look at Him' (p. 107). She then suggests that one should speak to him quite informally in one's own words. In all this St Teresa recommends gentleness and relaxation. 'In the early stages, then, one should strive to feel happy and free. There are some people who think that devotion will slip away from them if they relax a little.' (*Life*, p. 74).

It is for people in this Mansion that St John of the Cross recommends the discipline outlined in Book I of the *Ascent*, in which he describes the active night of the senses—those who have accepted the religious culture and count themselves Christian but who have little idea of the inner purgations which will be required if they are to enter farther into the Castle.

This is an important Mansion for it represents the first place of 'letting go', when the seed falls deep into the ground and the powers of *Yin* and *Yang* meet in creative tension. It is the time of Compline when the conscious will lets go into sleep allowing the unconscious to awaken, while at the same time, 'the adversary, the devil, as a roaring lion, walketh about, seeking whom he may devour'.

Up till now much of our response has been on a conscious level expressed in the things that we can do with reason and prudence in our own strength. And that is quite a lot. Such Christians, says St Teresa,

> are most desirous not to offend His Majesty; they avoid committing even venial sins; they love doing penance; they spend hours in recollection; they use their time well; they practise works of charity towards their neighbours . . . (*Interior Castle*, p. 221)

But in the cycle of the year they are still in the place of the Old Testament, of conflict between the Law and the flesh with its desires, which cannot be converted by morality alone. St Teresa introduces here the figure of the rich young man in the Gospel who was invited to let go of everything that gave him possession and control. Good works and rectitude will be of little use to the one who accepts the invitation, for God will release and bring to the surface those inner dispositions which need to be converted, of which he was previously unaware. This is frightening and confusing when he does not understand what is happening to him and so it may lead to long periods of aridity in prayer. Those who respond to this treatment with impatience, self-pity and resentment are showing that they lack the humility and self-knowledge to recognize their own need. St Teresa says to the nuns of her convent:

> Enter, then, enter within yourselves, my daughters; and get right away from your own trifling good works, for these you are bound, as Christians to perform, and, indeed, many more . . . Oh, humility, humility! . . . whenever I hear people making much of their times of aridity, I cannot help thinking that they are somewhat lacking in it. (p. 222)

In fact she sees the humility that will let go of its fears and rectitude in love as the only way of getting into the next Mansions.

> When we proceed with all this caution, we find stumbling-blocks everywhere; for we are afraid of everything, and so dare not go farther . . . for the love of the Lord, let us make a real effort: let us leave our reason and our fears in His hands, and let us forget the weakness of our nature which is apt to cause us so much worry. (*Interior Castle*, p. 226)

It is a journey of love and trust, and because Christ is not yet really alive for people in this Mansion they need help in the art of letting go—from a 'soul-friend' or an adviser of the right sort.

> It is a great advantage for us to be able to consult someone who knows us, so that we may learn to know ourselves. And it is a great encouragement to see that things which we thought impossible are possible to others... It makes us feel that we may emulate their flights and venture to fly ourselves, as the young birds do when their parents teach them. (p. 228)

Nowadays it may be that for some people, for some of the time, the adviser has to be a psychiatrist, for the ability to let go of fears and prejudices and to love may be impaired by psychological rather than spiritual causes. If the emotional apparatus through which the spiritual surrender has to be made is too damaged to function adequately, then it needs the healing skills which we would not deny to any other part of the human make-up. Psychology should be the handmaid of theology, not a substitute for it, and to expose oneself to the one as to the other will require all the humility and courage which St Teresa is advocating from within the culture and psychological climate of her day.

In this Mansion St Teresa recommends a form of prayer in which the image of Jesus, formerly pictured as standing outside the one who prays is brought within. She refers to it as the Prayer of Recollection and places it between the third and fourth Mansions as a preparation for the Prayer of Quiet.

> If one prays in this way, the prayer may be only vocal, but the mind will be recollected much sooner . . . It is called recollection because the soul collects together all the faculties and enters within itself to be with its God. Its Divine Master comes more speedily to teach it, and to grant it the Prayer of Quiet, than in any other way. For, hidden there within itself, it can think about the Passion, and picture the Son, and offer Him to the Father, without wearying the mind by going to seek Him on Mount Calvary, or in the Garden, or at the Column.
>
> (*Way of Perfection*, p. 115)

St Teresa (who is still recommending it in the sixth Mansion for those who find formal meditation impossible) enlarges on this form of prayer in the third Mansion as follows:

> A person involuntarily closes his eyes and desires solitude; and, without the display of any human skill, there seems to be gradually built up for him a temple in which he can make the prayer already described; the senses and all external things seem gradually to lose their hold on him, while the soul, on the other hand, regains its lost control.
>
> (*Interior Castle*, p. 240)

She insists that this kind of prayer is not something which can only be received, it can be practised.

> . . . you must understand that this is not a supernatural state but depends upon our volition, and that, by God's favour, we can enter it of our own accord: *this condition must be understood of everything that we say in this book can be done*, for without it nothing can be accomplished and we have not the power to think a single good thought. For this is not a silence of the faculties: it is a shutting-up of the faculties within itself by the soul. (*Way of Perfection*, pp. 120-1)

FOURTH MANSIONS: ENLIGHTENMENT

It is the hour of midnight when God himself works in the abyss through his incarnate Son. As the Church sings in the liturgy: 'While all things were in quiet silence and night was in the midst of her swift course, thine Almighty Word, O Lord, leaped down out of thy royal throne.' It is Christmas in the Church's year and in the Eucharist the point at which the Gospel is read. Within the new dispensation Christ, as a living person, begins to communicate himself directly to the individual in prayer. To understand what goes on in this Mansion one should bear in mind the distinctions already referred to in Chapter IV (pp. 21-2) between soul and spirit, and the fact that the spirit is often far ahead of the human faculties and those which man shares with the animal world. At the end of her chapters on the fourth Mansion St Teresa shows how sometimes the initial impact of spiritual reality is too much for the weak soul and body and that special care needs to be taken if one is to continue the journey in safety (pp. 245-6).

Her principal theme is that of the difference between spiritual sweetness, which comes largely through the psyche, and spiritual consolations, which are the result of the direct touch of Spirit upon spirit.

The difference is described in detail in *The Interior Castle* (pp. 231-3) and again under the image of the two fountains (pp. 236-8). In the case of spiritual sweetness the water

> comes from a long distance, by means of numerous conduits and through human skill . . . it reaches us by way of the thoughts; we meditate upon created things and fatigue the understanding; and when at last, by means of our own efforts, it comes, the satisfaction which it brings to the soul fills the basin, but in doing so makes a noise. (p.236-7)

The noise comes from the human emotions through which the spiritual communication passes:

> The spiritual sweetness . . . does not enlarge the heart; as a rule, it seems to oppress it somewhat. The soul experiences a great happiness when it realizes what it is doing for God's sake; but it sheds a few bitter tears which seem in some way to be the result of passion. (p. 232)

> . . . the tears and longings sometimes arise partly from our nature and from the state of preparedness we are in; but nevertheless, as I have said, they eventually lead one to God. (ibid.)

To the other fountain, that of spiritual consolations, 'the water comes direct from its source, which is God, and . . . its coming is accompanied by the greatest peace and quietness and sweetness within ourselves' (p. 237). Its effects are 'not felt, as earthly delights are felt, in the heart, but in the sense of 'the heart's being enlarged'. She quotes from Psalm 119:32 the words *dilatasti cor meum*, 'when thou hast enlarged my heart', to explain this sense which she does not actually feel has its source in the heart. 'It arises in a much more interior part, like something of which the springs are very deep; I think this must be the centre of the soul, as I have since realized' (p. 237).

Actual prayer at such a time will be very simple. 'The will, then, should be left to enjoy it, and should not labour except for uttering a few loving words' (p. 243).

St Teresa advises strongly against any attempt to produce the Prayer of Quiet by one's own efforts:

> . . . however much we may practise meditation, however much we do violence to ourselves, and however many tears we shed, we cannot produce this water in those ways; it is given only to whom God wills to give it and often when the soul is not thinking of it at all. (p. 239)

Neither should one try to produce silence artificially, by deliberate cessation of all activity in prayer. Rather,

> Let [the soul] try, without forcing itself or causing any turmoil, to put a stop to all discursive reasoning, yet not to suspend the understanding, nor to cease from all thought, though it is well for it to remember that it is in God's presence and Who this God is. If feeling this should lead it into a state of absorption, well and good; but it should not try to understand what this state is, because that is a gift bestowed upon the will. (*Interior Castle*, p. 243)

If the Prayer of Quiet is ***not*** given, then one should use the Prayer of Recollection which St Teresa also describes in the chapters concerning the fourth Mansions.

FIFTH MANSIONS: METANOIA AND RECONCILIATION

In each of the three diagrams this is a place which embraces night and morning, Passion and Resurrection, the death of the old that the new may grow. It is the daybreak of Resurrection life; for St Teresa, the beginning of union. The seed in the *I-Ching* circle lies still in its grave in apparent death until it is aroused and begins to grow in the form of a plant. Her favourite image in these chapters is that of the butterfly, symbol of the Resurrection, which lives because the silkworm has died in its cocoon. Her description is a résumé of the journey which has already been taken:

> The silkworm is like the soul which takes life when, through the heat which comes from the Holy Spirit, it begins to utilize the general help which God gives to us all, and to make use of the remedies which He left in His Church . . . The soul begins to live and nourishes itself on this food, and on good meditations, until it is full grown . . . then it starts to spin its silk and to build the house in which it is to die. This house may be understood here to mean Christ. I think I read or heard somewhere that our life is hid in Christ, or in God . . . (p. 254)

This passage confirms that until Christ is known to be living, so that his life can be shared, it is of little use to talk of 'dying' at any deeper level than that of discipline. For to die into a vacuum may be stoical or masochistic but it is not Christian. It is only when the third and fourth Mansions have been at least partially known that a simple obedience without psychological or intellectual supports and compensations can be fruitful, and the 'Come unto me' of Christ's first invitation can be extended to the 'Come follow me' of the life of union. So for St John of the Cross this is the place of the active night of the spirit because it involves the conversion of memory, understanding and will at a deeper level than that of the senses, to make possible a more simple following of Christ, without compensations.

St Teresa in the fifth Mansions describes two unions, one of prayer which continues and deepens in the next two Mansions, and the other of the will (p. 259-60). In prayer the 'direct touch' from God which is discussed in the fourth Mansions deepens and is accompanied by a sense of certainty which was not so apparent when the activities of spirit and psyche were more confused.

> God implants Himself in the interior of that soul in such a way that, when it returns to itself, it cannot possibly doubt that God has been in it and it has been in God; so firmly does this truth remain within it that, although for years God may never grant it that favour again, it can neither forget it nor doubt that it has received it . . . This certainty of the soul is very material. (p. 251)

The union of the will too is a deepening of what has been first known in the fourth Mansions in the experience of 'enlargement of heart'. One of the most certain signs that the prayer of union has been experienced is that self-concern is giving place to a concern for God's honour and glory, for his interests and those of others (p. 257-8). This is coupled with a practical love of one's neighbour because he is loved by God.

> But here the Lord asks only two things of us: love for His Majesty and love for our neighbour. It is for these two virtues that we must strive, and if we attain them perfectly we are doing His will and so shall be united with Him . . . The surest sign that we are keeping these two commandments is, I think, that we should really be loving our neighbour; for we cannot be sure if we are loving God, although we may have good reasons for believing that we are, but we can know quite well if we are loving our neighbour. And be certain that, the farther advanced you find you are in this, the greater the love you will have for God. (p. 261)

So it is the union of the will with the will of God which is the essential factor, while experiences of union in prayer are a free gift from him.

St Teresa warns that temptations in these Mansions will be of a much more subtle kind, with the devil using undermining tactics to seduce the one who has already come such a long way. In terms of marriage imagery one must not yet consider oneself united with the bridegroom, for neither spiritual marriage nor betrothal have yet taken place. It is as if two people were spending short periods of time together, getting to know one another at a more intimate level (p. 264-5). Care must be taken to develop the relationship, for the periods of union in prayer as in life are probably known only for short stretches of time.

SIXTH MANSIONS: MYSTICAL UNION

These Mansions belong pre-eminently to the Holy Spirit. In the *I-Ching* circle the gentle Spring breezes bring the plant to its full growth. It is the hour of Pentecost, of the Office of Terce and of the coming of the Holy Spirit upon the reconciled soul to bring it to perfection. In eleven chapters St Teresa deals with the possibilities which may be, but not necessarily are, realized when the Spirit comes with his gifts to the soul. St Paul says that there are many different gifts which seem to be distributed quite arbitrarily, and the kind of things which happened in sixteenth-century Spain need not necessarily occur in twentieth-century England. However, St Teresa is quite clear that it is by no means necessary to salvation to have experienced any of the more dramatic of these gifts. She says:

> And let none of you imagine that, because a Sister has had such experiences, she is any better than the rest; the Lord leads each of us as He sees we have need. Such experiences, if we use them aright, prepare us to be better servants of God; but sometimes it is the weakest whom God leads by this road; and so there is no ground here for approval or for condemnation. We must base our judgments on the virtues. (p. 314)

As we saw in the previous Mansions, the spirit goes ahead and receives tokens of union which in fact amount to nothing unless they lead to a resolution of the will to become more united with the will of God, which is the true spiritual betrothal. This betrothal is described in the image of two wax candles which can be 'joined so that the light they give is one . . . yet afterwards the one candle can be perfectly well separated from the other and the candles become two again' (p. 335). So these mystical experiences, designed to arouse the inmost will of the one who prays, may come and go, but will eventually lead to a union in which all his faculties are embraced. Briefly these special gifts may be placed under four headings:

a) Locutions of three kinds: (i) corporeal, such as Samuel heard as a child in the Temple; (ii) imaginary, which are not heard by the physical ear but the impression gained is of the same kind; and (iii) intellectual, where a spiritual truth is, as it were, planted in the depths of the spirit without outward sound or voice but with a sense of certainty.

b) Raptures, ecstasies and trances, including suspension of breathing, a sense of the flight of the spirit, and of being pierced by an arrow of love and the pain of fire.

c) Intellectual visions (often considered to be the purest form) in which there is consciousness of the Lord's nearness, or of some truth of the faith without anything being seen or felt by the senses.

d) Imaginary visions. Here there is an actual vision either of Christ's sacred humanity or of some other truth. 'Although He does this so quickly that we might liken the action to a flash of lightning, this most glorious image is so deeply engraven upon the imagination that I do not believe it can possibly disappear until it is seen where it can be enjoyed to all eternity' (*Interior Castle*, p. 315).

Careful examination will show that apart from the raptures and ecstasies and (if one is not a fundamentalist) the corporeal locutions, there is little here that should cause difficulty. They are phenomena which are experienced at one time or another by many Christians and not necessarily by those advanced in holiness.*

---

*An example of an intellectual vision is recorded in *Woman in a Man's World*, the autobiography of Rosamund Essex, formerly editor of *The Church Times*, who experienced it when she was only a nominal Christian. 'I was alone in the house one night in a lighted room and I opened the door to a passage where there were no lights on—just dense darkness. I was not thinking of anything in particular. As I opened the door, *God was on the other side*. It was like a great blow in the face, so strong that it took my breath away. I stood stunned. I suppose that I waited there for a second or so; and then there was the door and the darkness beyond and nothing else. But something had happened and nothing could make me

St Teresa puts these gifts into perspective in three ways. Firstly, despite the rapture, the experiences are not all joy; they are accompanied by so many trials and sufferings that only the courage that God gives will enable one to bear them. Secondly, the important seventh chapter emphasizes the need always to keep in touch with the humanity of our Lord through simple meditation of the kind recommended in the third Mansions as the Prayer of Recollection. The special manifestations of the Spirit's action come and go, and meanwhile the bread and butter on which the soul is nourished must be that of meditation. 'If anyone told me that she experienced them continuously (I mean so continuously that she could never meditate in the way I have described) I should consider it suspicious' (p. 308). Thirdly, the genuineness of the gifts is known by their fruits, the desire both for solitude and for the apostolate which are signs of the effects of divine love.

> The soul would like to flee from other people, and greatly envies those who live, or who have lived, in deserts. On the other hand it would like to plunge right into the heart of the world, to see if by doing this it could help one soul to praise God more . . . (p. 298)

So the things which happen in this Mansion cannot be equated with the happy, peaceful absorption of the Prayer of Quiet experienced in the fourth Mansions.

One can place St John's passive night of the spirit here alongside St Teresa's teaching, although his treatment of the subject is somewhat different. He does not deny the validity of charismatic gifts, but distinguishes between the inner imprint of them on the soul and their outward manifestations.

> . . . the good that overflows in the soul from supernatural apprehensions, when they come from a good source, is produced passively in the soul at that very instant when they are represented to the senses, without the working of any operation of the faculties. Wherefore it is unnecessary for the will to perform the act of receiving them . . . Nay,

---

believe that it had not . . . I began to come back to faith little by little—to a new kind of faith which did not depend solely on what other people had taught me, but was mine, bright and shining.' I would consider this to be a spiritual rather than a paranormal experience, because its fruits were Rosamund's conversion.

> rather, as the spirituality coming from those imaginary apprehensions is given passively to the soul, even so must the soul conduct itself passively with respect to them, setting no store by its inward or outward actions. (*Ascent*, III. xiii. 3)

This passage comes in the section in which St John is writing of the active night of the spirit because, in his opinion, the outer signs can and should be negated if the inner message is to do its work. The gift is to be received in silence and passivity and one should neither know nor attempt to judge what has been given. *This* is the passive night which will prepare the soul for union, and if St John underlines the trials of the way in the second book of *The Dark Night* while St Teresa stresses the joys and the privileges, they both know that in it the soul is being purified by something which cannot be self-induced.

SEVENTH MANSIONS: COMMUNION, MISSION

This is the place of union. The flower opens and is drenched in the light and heat of high noon; other creatures see and fertilize it and from this service fruit is formed which in its turn will serve the earth and the species. In the Eucharist it is the time of communion to be followed by dismissal into the world for service or martyrdom. For St Teresa it is the time of spiritual marriage which she describes sometimes in terms of a bridal relationship and sometimes in terms of absorption. 'Here it is like rain falling from the heavens into a river or a spring; there is nothing but water there and it is impossible to divide or separate the water belonging to the river from that which fell from the heavens' (*Interior Castle*, p. 335).

Yet the imagery of light, communion and mission prevails. She expresses the inner state as one in which the image of the Trinity is restored in the soul.

> It sees these three Persons individually, and yet, by a wonderful kind of knowledge which is given to it, the soul realizes that most certainly and truly all these three Persons are one Substance and one Power and one Knowledge and one God alone; so that what we hold by faith the soul may be said here to grasp by sight, although nothing is seen by the eyes, either of the body or of the soul . . . Here all three Persons communicate Themselves to the soul and speak to the soul and explain to it those words which the Gospel attributes to the Lord—namely, that He

> and the Father and the Holy Spirit will come to dwell with the soul which loves Him and keeps His commandments. (p. 331-2)

This was completed for Teresa by a vision of the Lord, who revealed himself to her in his humanity

> when she had just received Communion, in great splendour and beauty and majesty, as He did after His resurrection, and told her that it was time she took upon her His affairs as if they were her own and that He would take her affairs upon Himself. (p. 334)

All the raptures and excitements of the previous Mansions have died down because 'the instantaneous communication of God to the soul' no longer comes through the faculties or senses but in a more organic way. Every part of one's being has now been drawn into union so that there is nothing left outside to react noisily as it once did to the intrusion of a strange thing. Below the trials and difficulties of daily life all is at peace, yet there is no absolute security as one can experience even here the reptiles of the first Mansions (cf. p. 341-4).

Union has the effect of making the one who experiences it progressively more outgoing, for as the life of the Trinity must of its nature flow out to creatures, so also will the life of the Christian as it is drawn closer to God. St Teresa says that one may think

> that such a person will not remain in possession of her senses but will be so completely absorbed that she will be able to fix her mind upon nothing. But no: in all that belongs to the service of God she is more alert than before; and, when not otherwise occupied, she rests in that happy companionship. (p. 332)

St Teresa goes on to list the effects of union. These include self-forgetfulness: 'So entirely is she employed in seeking the honour of God' that 'she seems no longer to exist . . . save when she realizes that she can do something to advance the glory and honour of God' (p. 339). There is a desire for suffering, but not of a masochistic kind:

> This is not of such a kind as to disturb the soul, as it did previously. So extreme is her longing for the will of God to be done in her that whatever His Majesty does she considers to be for the best: if He wills that she should suffer, well and good; if not, she does not worry herself to death as she did before. (p. 339)

There is the typical mark of the saint—love for one's enemies:

> When these souls are persecuted again, they have a great interior joy . . . They bear no enmity to those who ill-treat them, or desire to do so. Indeed they conceive a special love for them, so that, if they see them in some trouble, they are deeply grieved and would do anything possible to relieve them. (p. 339)

The whole person is strengthened in his humanity:

> It cannot be doubted that, if we are made one with the Strong, we shall gain strength through the most sovereign union of spirit with Spirit, and we shall appreciate the strength of the saints which enabled them to suffer and die . . . It is quite certain that, with the strength it has gained, the soul comes to the help of all who are in the Castle, and, indeed, succours the body itself. (p. 347)

Good works are the fruit and test of prayer:

> This, my daughters, is the aim of prayer: this is the purpose of the Spiritual Marriage, of which are born good works and good works alone. Such works, as I have told you, are the sign of every genuine favour and of everything else that comes from God. (p. 346)

Here St Teresa is very realistic indeed. One starts where one is, with the people near at hand, not with ambitious schemes for teaching and preaching (which in any case were impossible for women in her day). It is the magnitude of the love which counts and which is used in union with that of Christ to do far more than the triviality of most of one's actions would warrant.

> In a word, my sisters, I will end by saying that we must not build towers without foundations, and that the Lord does not look so much at the magnitude of anything we do as the love with which we do it. If we accomplish what we can, His Majesty will see to it that we become able to do more each day. We must not begin by growing weary; but during the whole of this short life, which for any one of you may be shorter than you think, we must offer the Lord whatever interior and exterior sacrifice we are able to give Him, and His Majesty will unite it with that which He offered to the Father for us upon the Cross, so that it may have the value won for it by our will, even though our actions in themselves may be trivial. (p. 350)

It may well be asked how anyone who has reached this point needs to enter again into those Mansions which have been left behind. In a sense, St Teresa answers this question in her Epilogue to *The Interior Castle*:

> Although I have spoken here only of seven Mansions, yet *in each* there are comprised many more, both above and below and around, with lovely gardens and fountains and things so delectable that you will want to lose yourself in praise of the great God . . . (p. 351)

It is assumed that the inmost rooms of the Castle are reached before death, yet even after having experienced the seventh Mansion it is necessary to go on living and growing. What has happened during the first journey into the Castle has been a gradual transference of the whole self, body, mind and spirit, into the life of Jesus. This will not have been a steady progression, but a matter of steps taken backwards as well as forwards, with certain Mansions bypassed and others dwelt in for a very long time. Although the transference in terms of prayer and living may seem to have begun in the fourth Mansion, yet the preceding Mansions have been places of preparation in which the tradition has been learnt and practised. After this, growth in awareness, deepening understanding, the response to new facets of life at a particular resting-point, will continue until death and perhaps beyond. Henceforward, however, the way will be more flexible and it may well be that some Mansions need never be entered again.

PRINCIPAL EVENTS IN THE LIFE OF ST TERESA

1515 Teresa de Ahumada born at Avila in Spain.

1536 Entered the Carmelite Convent of the Incarnation, Avila, under the Mitigated Rule. She always regarded the following twenty years as a period of semi-conversion.

1556-7 Final 'conversion'. First contact with the Society of Jesus.

1562 Founded the first convent of the Reform, St Joseph's in Avila, under the 13th-century Primitive Rule of St Albert. Lived there until 1567. Drew up her own Constitutions.

1565 Greater part of the *Life* written in its final version. *The Way of Perfection* begun.

1567 Authorization by the Carmelite General for the foundation of further convents of the Reform. Primitive Rule and Constitutions approved.

1568 Teresa assisted in the foundation of the first Discalced Carmelite Friary in Duruelo with St John of the Cross and Fr Antonio of Jesus.

1562-82 Founded Discalced Carmelite convents throughout Spain.

1573 Began to write the *Foundations*. (Completed in 1582.)

1577 *The Interior Castle* written. (Revised in 1580.)

1582 Died in October at Alba de Tormes.

PRINCIPAL EVENTS IN THE LIFE OF ST JOHN OF THE CROSS

1542 Juan de Yepes born at Fontiveros near Avila.

1559 Studied at the Jesuit College in Medino del Campo.

1563-4 Took the Carmelite habit in the priory of Santa Ana, Medina del Campo. Made his profession. Entered the University of Salamanca.

1567 Ordained priest. Met St Teresa and agreed to join the first Discalced Friary of the Reform.

1568 Became one of the first three Friars at Duruelo, taking the vows of the Reform as Fr John of the Cross.

1572 Went as confessor to the Convent of the Incarnation at Avila where St Teresa was prioress.

1577 Kidnapped by the Calced Carmelites and imprisoned at Toledo. Began to write *The Spiritual Canticle*. Escaped.

1578-9 Confessor to the Discalced Carmelite nuns at Beas. Wrote much of his poetry, began to write *The Ascent of Mount Carmel* and prose commentary on *The Spiritual Canticle*.

1579-81 Rector of the new Carmelite college at Baeza.

1580-81 The Discalced Carmelites recognized as a separate province by the Pope. St John made third definitor of the Order and prior at Granada. Most of his prose works were written at this time. Visited St Teresa at Avila eleven months before her death.

1585 Rise of Nicolas Doria, a rigorous administrator, as provincial. St John made vicar-provincial of Andalusia. In the next two years made many new foundations.

1588 Made first definitor of the Discalced congregation. In August, prior of Segovia and deputy-general for Doria.

The next few years brought growing difficulties between Doria and St John, culminating in the General Chapter of June 1591 when St John was deprived of his offices and sent to a priory near Baeza where he fell ill.

1591 Died at Ubeda in December.